Count The Leprechauns & More!

The St. Patricks Day Counting Experience For Children Aged 2 - 6!

From the authors of the best-selling book...

BEST OF LUCK!

HOW MANY LEPRECHAUNS CAN YOU COUNT?

THERE ARE TWO LEPRECHAUNS!

1

2

Leprechauns are little Irish, mythological fairies!

COUNT THE POTS OF GOLD!

1 2 3 4

THERE ARE FOUR!

Did you find your pot of gold
at the end of the rainbow yet?

HOW MANY RAINBOWS ARE THERE HERE?

THERE IS JUST **ONE** RAINBOW!

1

Did you count correctly?

ARE THERE MORE **THREE** OR MORE **FOUR LEAF CLOVERS?**

THERE ARE...

3 THREE LEAF CLOVERS

4 FOUR LEAF CLOVERS

So, there are more four leaf
clovers than three leaf clovers! Isn't that <u>lucky</u>!

COUNT THE PURPLE

FLOWERS

......1, 2, 3

PURPLE FLOWERS

1

2

3

Are there MORE GOLD OR GREEN GEMS?

THERE ARE **EIGHT** GREEN GEMS

 **8**

AND **SIX** GOLD GEMS!

6

Which means there are more green gems than golden gems!

Can you count how many harps there are?

1

THERE IS ONLY ONE HARP!

Harps Fact:

HOW MANY **PADDIES DAY** **DOGS** CAN YOU COUNT?

1   **2**   **3**

THAT'S **THREE** ST. PATRICKS DAY DOGS!

Do you have any pet dogs
at your house?

HOW MANY PAIRS OF BELLS ARE THERE?

(HINT: A PAIR MEANS TWO OF THE SAME THING, TOGETHER)

1

FIVE PAIRS OF BELLS!

3

2

4

5

HOW MANY **MUSHROOMS** ARE THERE?

WOW, THERE ARE **SEVEN** MUSHROOMS!

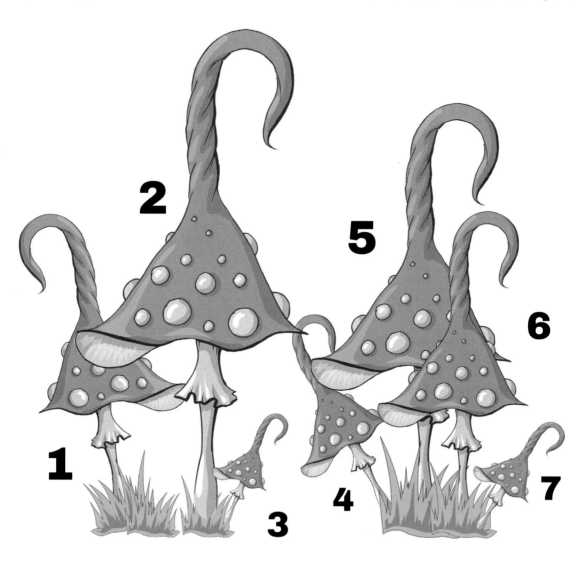

Are there MORE CLOVERS or MORE IRISH FLAGS?

THERE ARE **TEN** IRISH FLAGS

 **10**

AND **FIVE** CLOVERS!

5

Which means there are more flags than clovers, did you count correctly?

HOW MANY HAPPY LEPRECHAUNS ARE THERE?

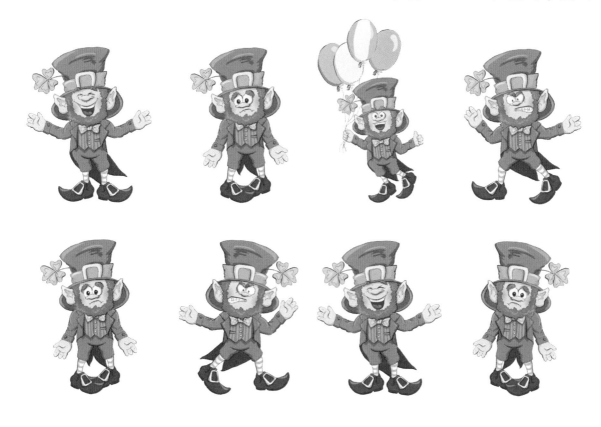

THREE OF THE LEPRECHAUNS ARE HAPPY – THE OTHER FIVE WERE SAD OR ANGRY!

1

2

3

HOW MANY OF THE CHILDREN ARE GIRLS?

THERE ARE **FIVE** GIRLS!

1

Hopefully you counted the right number!

COUNT THE LEPRECHAUN HATS!

THE ANSWER IS **TWO LEPRECHAUN HATS**

2

Did you count the correct number?

IN TOTAL, HOW MANY RAINBOWS

ARE THERE IN THE ENTIRE BOOK?

(INCLUDING THE ONE ON THIS PAGE, AND ALL THOSE ON ANSWER PAGES!)

IN THE WHOLE BOOK, THERE ARE

10
RAINBOWS

DON'T FORGET TO BUY THE EXTREMELY POPULAR 'COUNT THE CARS' ON AMAZON! WE'D ALSO REALLY APPRECIATE IF YOU CAN LEAVE A 5* REVIEW IF YOU ENJOYED TEACHING YOUR CHILD WITH THIS BOOK!

Made in the USA
Middletown, DE
13 March 2020